Ballads of Battle

Lance-Corporal Joseph Lee

(1876-1949)

Bill Bruce.

Blenheim House
MELKSHAM
Wilts

BIBLIOLIFE

BALLADS OF BATTLE

BY LANCE-CORPORAL JOSEPH LEE
1ST/4TH BATTALION BLACK WATCH

WITH ILLUSTRATIONS BY THE AUTHOR

LONDON
JOHN MURRAY, ALBEMARLE STREET, W.
1916

WILLIAM BRENDON AND SON, LIMITED, PRINTERS
PLYMOUTH, ENGLAND

TO
MY COMRADES
IN ARMS

CONTENTS

CONTENTS

LIST OF ILLUSTRATIONS

CORPORAL, 69TH PUNJABIS

I writ these songs in a dead man's book ;
I stole the strain from a dead man's look ;
And if much of death there may seem to be
'Tis because the dead are so dear to me.

THE HALF-HOUR'S FURLOUGH

I THOUGHT that a man went home last
   night
   From the trench where the tired men
   lie,
And walked through the streets of his own
   old town—
   And I thought that the man was I.

And I walked through the gates of that
   good old town
   Which circles below the hill,
And laves its feet in the river fair
   That floweth so full and still.

Gladly and gladly into my heart
   Came the old street sounds and sights,
And pleasanter far than the Pleiades
   Was the gleam of the old street lights.

And as I came by St. Mary's Tower,
  The old, solemn bell struck ten,
And back to me echoed the memory
  Of my boyhood days again :
Musing I turned me East about
  To the haunt of my fellow-men.

There were some that walked, and some
    that talked,
  Beneath the old Arcade,
And for comfort I elbowed among the
    throng
  And hearkened to what they said.

Some were that talked, and some that
    walked
  By one, by two, by three ;
And some there were who spake my name
  As though they lovéd me.

And some who said, " Might he but return
  When this weary war is spent ! "
And it moved me much that their thought
    was such,
  And I turned me well content.

I passed me along each familiar way,
   And paused at each friendly door,
And thought of the things that had
    chanced within
   In the kindly days of yore.

Till I came to the place of my long, long
    love,
   Where she lay with her head on her
    arm ;
And she sighed a prayer that the dear
    Lord should
   Shield my body from all harm.

Ae kiss I left on her snow-white brow,
   And ane on her raven hair,
And ane, the last, on her ruby lips,
   Syne forth again I fare.

And I came to the home that will aye be
    home,
   And brightly the fires did burn,
And at hearth, and in hearts, was a place
    for me
   'Gainst the day that I should return.

Then I came to the glade where my mother
    was laid,
  'Neath the cypress and the yew :
And she stood abune, and she said, " My
    son,
  I am glad that your heart was true."

And I passed me over both hill and down,
  By each well-remembered path,
While the blessed dawn, like the love o'
    God,
  Stole over the sleeping Strath.

And from a thorn came the pipe of a
    thrush,
  Like the first faint pipes of Peace :
It slid with healing into my heart,
  And my sorrowing found surcease.

*   *   *   *   *

Then I awoke to the sound of guns,
  And in my ears was the cry :
" The Second Relief will stand to arms ! "
  And I rose—for that man was I.

MACFARLANE'S DUG-OUT

"This is the house that Mac built."

SINCE the breed that were our forebears
    first crouched within a cave,
And found their food and fought their foe
    with arrow and with stave,
And the things that really mattered unto
    men were four, or three :
Shelter, and sustenance ; a maid ; the
    simple right to be ;
And Fear stalked through the forest and
    slid adown the glade—
There's been nothing like the dug-out
    that Macfarlane made !

When Mac first designed his dug-out,
    and commenced his claim to peg,
He thought of something spacious in
    which one might stretch a leg,

Might lie out at one's leisure, and sit up
    at one's ease,
And not be butted in the back by t'other
    fellow's knees ;
Of such a goodly fashion were the plans
    the builder laid,
And even so the dug-out that Macfarlane
    made.

He shored it up with timber, and he
    roofed it in with tin
Torn from the battered boxes that they
    bring the biscuits in—
(He even used the biscuits, but he begs I
    should not state
The number that he took for tiles, the
    number that he ate !)—
He shaped it, and secured it to withstand
    the tempest's shocks—
(I know he stopped one crevice with the
    latest gift of socks !)—
He trimmed it with his trenching-tool,
    and slapped it with his spade—
A marvel was the dug-out that Macfarlane
    made.

MACFARLANE IN HIS DUG-OUT

A Portrait Sketch

B

He lined the walls with sand-bags, and he
laid the floor with wood,
And when his eye beheld it, he beheld it
very good ;
A broken bayonet in a chink to hold the
candle-light ;
A waterproof before the door to keep all
weather-tight ;
A little shelf for bully, butter, bread, and
marmalade—
Then finished was the dug-out that Macfarlane made.

Except the Lord do build the house there
is no good or gain ;
Except the Lord keeps ward with us the
watchman wakes in vain :
So when we'd passed the threshold, and
partaken of Mac's tea,
And chalked upon the lintel, " At the
Back o' Bennachie,"
Perchance a prayer soared skyward,
although no word was said—
At least, God blessed the dug-out that
Macfarlane made !

For when the night was dark with dread,
   and the day was red with death,
And the whimper of the speeding steel
   passed like a shuddering breath,
And the air was thick with wingéd war,
   riven shard, and shrieking shell,
And all the earth did spit and spume like
   the cauldron hot of Hell :
When the heart of man might falter, and
   his soul be sore afraid—
We just dived into the dug-out that Macfarlane made !*

Deep is the sleep I've had therein, as free
   from sense of harm,
As when my curly head was laid in the
   crook of my mother's arm ;
My old great-coat for coverlet, curtain,
   and counterpane,
While patter, patter on the roof, came the
   shrapnel lead like rain ;

* It may interest the reader to know that these
lines are being written during a very considerable
bombardment, in which one misses the friendly
proximity of just such a dug-out as Macfarlane's.

And when a huge " Jack Johnson " made
    us a sudden raid,
I was dug out from the dug-out that
    Macfarlane made !

If in the unseen scheme of things, as well
    may be, it chance
That I bequeath my body to the soil of
    sunny France,
I will not cavil though they leave me
    sleeping where I fell,
With just a little wooden cross my lowly
    tale to tell :
I do not ask for sepulture beneath some
    cypress shade—
Just a six by two feet " dug-out " by
    Macfarlane made.

Postscript.—In the trenches, as will be readily
understood, one has no continual abiding place.
Consequently the dug-out of the picture is not the
dug-out of the poem, and when last I looked in
upon Macfarlane, he was swinging contentedly in a
hammock of his own construction. It unfortunately
falls to me to add a postscript of sadder import.
Since the Advance of 25th September, my comrade
has been counted among the missing.

FREIMDUN DHU :
THE BLACK WATCH

Betwixt 1715 and 1745 several independent companies were raised to secure the pacification of the
Highlands. From the dark character of the tartans
worn by most of the composing clans the companies
became known as the Freimdun Dhu, or Black
Watch, in contradistinction to the Leidman Diarag,
or Red Soldiers. After their embodiment into a
regiment of the line, no clan having a supreme
claim to impress its tartan upon the whole, and the
Colonel, Lord Crawford, being a Lowlander, the
peculiarly dark pattern still worn was devised.

Dark is thy tartan, Freimdun Dhu ;
Black and green, and green and blue :

Now in it I see thread of red—
The blood our Highland host has shed.

MY RIFLE

To the humour, and the good humour, of the genial sergeant I owe it that the period of my early drilling, which might thinkably have been a time of deadly dullness, afforded me much entertainment, as well as not a little valuable instruction. The sergeant was always at his best in dilating upon the virtues of the rifle, and the necessity for treating it with respect.

I'M the Soldier's surest friend :
I will neither break nor bend.

Straight and sterling, tried and true ;
You keep me and I'll keep you.

Bolt and barrel, butt and band ;
Caress me with a careful hand.

Stock and swivel, sling and sight ;
Rub me down, and keep me right.

Striker, trigger, cocking-piece ;
Give 'em all some elbow-grease.

SERGEANT J. CALLARY

Clean me clean, and oil me well ;
I'll kill your man and never tell.

Leave me dirty, oil me ill ;
You're the chap I'm going to kill.

Leave me lying all awry ;
You're the feller's going to die.

Daily do but pull me through ;
I will do the same for you.

Only use a " two by four "—
Nothing less, and nothing more.

" Pull-through " rag will do the trick ;
A shirt or sock is going to stick !

And keep your bottle full of ile—
Remember the Virgins' parabile !

Handle me with care, I beg,
I'm not so stout as old Mons Meg !

Do not pitch me on the ground—
To break me, a hammer can be found !

The soldier doesn't clean his rifle
Has 'listed with intent to trifle.

The chap who doesn't clean his gun
Is sorriest soldier 'neath the sun.

I'm the Soldier's surest friend :
I will neither break nor bend.

Straight and sterling, tried and true—
You keep me and I'll keep you.

THE DEAD MAN

HE lay unasking of our aid,
   His grim face questioning the sky,
While we stood by with idle spade,
   And gazed on him with curious eye.

Upon one hand a little ring ;
   A little earth clutched in one hand,
As he would bear some kindly thing
   Unto that new and unknown land.

This unnamed heap of human dust,
   Buoyant so late with human breath,
And now majestic and august
   With th' vast indifference of death !

Within that many-mansioned brain,
   A-through its corridors and cells,
Do no ghosts flit ? Comes ne'er again
   Old Memory with her mystic spells ?

Do images of wife or child
   Round these unseeing eyes still hover ?
Still heart, comes there no stirring wild,
   No cry for her might be thy lover ?

Nay, silence alone doth clothe thy clay,
   Thy mien is big with only mystery ;
No hieroglyphics here to say
   Where was thy home, and what thy
     history.

A chilly wind stirs in the grass ;
   There comes the night-jar's shrilling cry;
I see no recognition pass
   Into thy once beholding eye.

Comes the grim converse of a gun,
   But brings thee neither fear nor frown ;
Thou for thyself a Peace hast won,
   The bundle of thy life laid down.

Into its cell thy clay we thrust,
   And turn, and find we have no tears :
Deep be thy sleep, O once dear dust,
   Through the intolerable years !

THE PENITENT

As I lay in the trenches at Noove Chapelle,
Where the big guns barked like the
   Hounds o' Hell,
Sez I to mysel', sez I to mysel' :—

Billy, me boy, here's the end o' you—
But if, by good luck, ye should chance to
   slip thro',
Ye'll bid all ye'r evil companions adieu ;
Keep the Lord's ten Commands—and
   Lord Kitchener's two—
     Sez I to mysel'—at Noove Chapelle.

No more women, and no more wine,
No more hedgin' to get down the line,
No more hoggin' around like a swine,
     After Noove Chapelle—sez I to mysel'.

But only the good God in Heaven knows
The wayward way that a soldier goes,
And He must ha' left me to walk by my-
sel'—
 For three times I've fell, since Noove
 Chapelle.

Once at Bethune and twice at Estaires,
The divil gripped hould o' me unawares—
Yet often and often I've prayed me
prayers,
 Since I prayed by mysel', at Noove
 Chapelle.

Well, the Lord above, who fashioned the
French,
May bethink how bewitchin' is wine and a
wench
To a chap that's been tied for three weeks
to a trench,
 Around Noove Chapelle—that black
 border o' Hell.

And me throat was dry and the night was
  damp,
And the rum was raw—and red was the
  lamp !—
And—Billy, me boy, ye'r a bit o' a scamp,
    That's the truth to tell—tho' I sez it
      mysel'.

What's worritin' me isn't fear that they'll
  miss
Me out o' the ranks in the realms o' bliss ;
It ain't hope o' Heaven, nor horror o' Hell,
But just breakin' the promise, 'twixt God
  and mysel',
    Made at Noove Chapelle.

Well, there's always a way that is open to
  men
When they gets the knock-out—that's get
  up again ;
And, sure now, ould Satan ain't yet
  counted ten !
I'm game for another good bout wi' mysel'—
    As at Noove Chapelle.

THE BULLET

EVERY bullet has its billet ;
  Many bullets more than one :
God ! Perhaps I killed a mother
  When I killed a mother's son.

THE GREEN GRASS

THE dead spake together last night,
    And one to the other said :
    " *Why are we dead ?* "

They turned them face to face about
    In the place where they were laid :
    " Why are we dead ? "

" This is the sweet, sweet month o' May,
    And the grass is green o'erhead—
    Why are we dead ?

" The grass grows green on the long, long tracks
    That I shall never tread—
    Why are we dead ?

" The lamp shines like the glow-worm spark,
    From the bield where I was bred—
    Why am I dead ? "

The other spake : " I've wife and weans,
    Yet I lie in this waesome bed—
    Why am I dead ?

" O, I hae wife and weans at hame,
    And they clamour loud for bread—
    Why am I dead ? "

Quoth the first : " I have a sweet, sweet
    heart,
    And this night we should hae wed—
    Why am I dead ?

" And I can see another man
    Will mate her in my stead,
    Now I am dead."

They turned them back to back about
    In the grave where they were laid :—
    " Why are we dead ? "

" I mind o' a field, a foughten field,
    Where the bluid ran routh and red—
    Now I am dead."
    c

" I mind o' a field, a stricken field,
    And a waeful wound that bled—
    Now I am dead."

They turned them on their backs again,
    As when their souls had sped,
    And nothing further said.

    *   *   *   *   *

The dead spake together last night,
    And each to the other said,
    " *Why are we dead ?* "

STAND-TO !

I'D just crawled into me dug-out,
  And pulled me coat over me 'ead,
    When the Corpor-al
    He begins to bawl,
And these were the words he said :
    " Stand-to——
Show a leg !—Get a move on, You !—
    Ye's can't lie and snore,
    Till the end o' the war—
Stand-to !—STAND-TO !   STAND-TO ! "

I was just a-dreamin' of 'Ome Sweet 'Ome,
  A-top of a fevver bed ;
    And Sister Nell
    Had looked in to tell
Of tea, and of toasted bread—
    "Stand-to ! "—
Of a sudden a change of view—
    " Come on—you there—
    Take a sniff o' fresh air—
Stand-to !—STAND-TO !   STAND-TO ! "

25

AT THE DAWN

A Drama of the Trenches.

ORION raised his red right hand
  As marshalling the starry host :
Below I took my lonely stand,
  Somewhere anigh the Lonely Post.

Orion wheels adown the sky ;
  A broken moon to Westward wends,
While I cast up a wistful eye,
  Counting the stars among my friends ;

Counting each burning bead that hung
  Suspend in that great rosary
Which makes, unto the Might that flung,
  An Orison continually.

And then the broken moon went out,
  And one by one went out the stars,
And, welcome as a friendly shout,
  Dawn broke from out her prison bars.

26

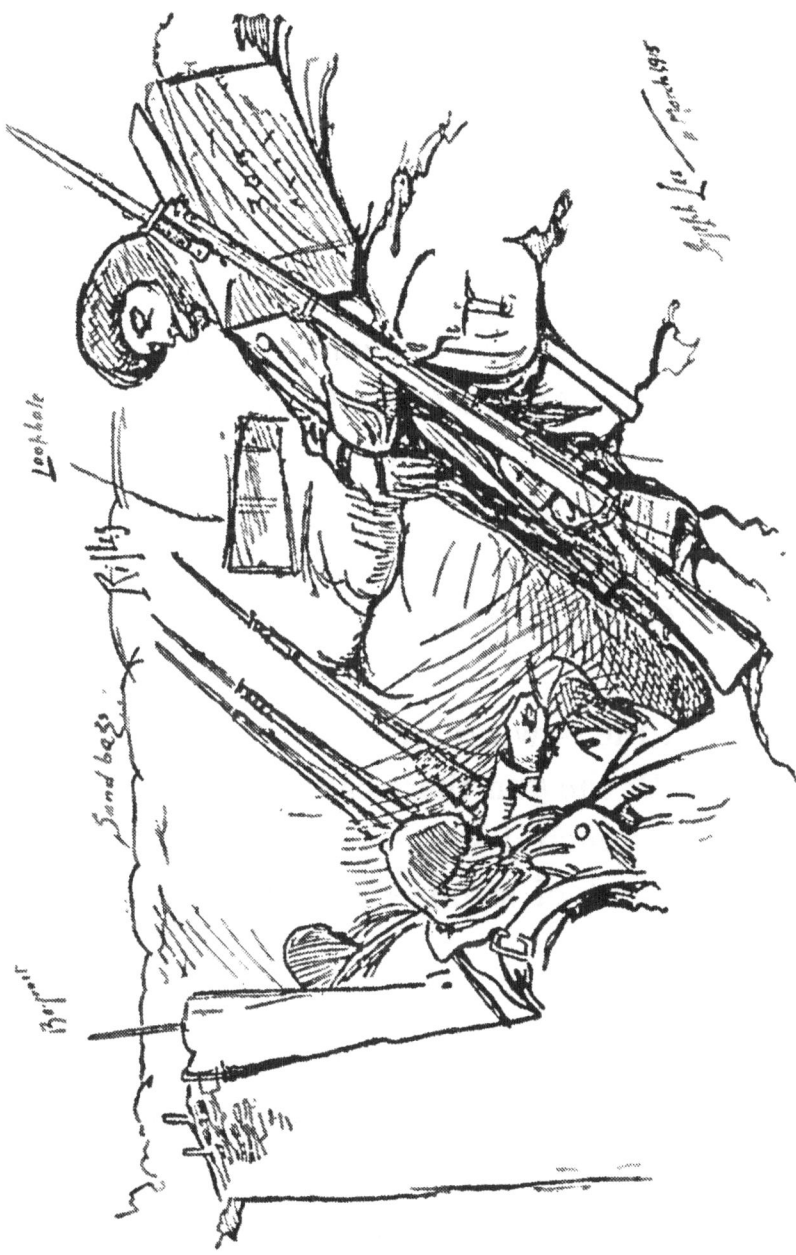

DAWN IN THE TRENCHES

An unfinished drawing made on the morning after Neuve Chapelle.

As Lazarus risen from the dead.——"At the Dawn."

C 2

But such a dawn as might have been
   Prelude to an horrific play ;
As if some Scientist had foreseen
   The diverse drama of the day.

A dawn of streaks and streams of red,
   Like swelling gouts of spilten blood ;
Blood-red the sun that raised its head
   Above the broken, blasted wood :
As Lazarus risen from the dead,
   Silent each dust-clad sentry stood.

And with the dawn there came a gun,
   And with the gun there came a cry ;
Along the trench it seemed to run
   That sound of strong men when they
     die.

Then one came running in all haste,
   With, " Water, water, for Christ's
     sake ! "
I hitched the bottle from my waist
   And marvelled how his hand did shake.

I saw the shaking of his hand,
   Which dripped with blood was not his
      own :
I saw each drop merge with the sand,
   Like seed some Evil One had sown.

Then he was gone, and I stood there,
   Still gazing on the reddened ground,
And musing whether wheat or tare
   From such a sowing would be found.

And there was silence for a space,
   Save that a lark sang on the wing ;
Then, crouching low, with grim-set
      face,
   Up the long trench came Hira Singh.

He paused by me, and with a blow
   He struck the stopper in his flask,
And told me what I sought to know
   Before my tongue had time to ask.

He told me what I sought to know
Before my tongue had time to ask.

—"At the Dawn."

" Finished ! " he said, and closed his eyes,
  As he had closed those of the dead ;
And twice he snored, as one who tries
  To breathe through blood: "Finished!"
    he said.

  *   *   *   *   *

A soldier's cross stood in the corn,
  A simple cross as one might see :
Bethought me of that other morn
  That broke o'er barren Calvary.

And of the word the Christ had cried
  When His long agony was done :
The " It is finished ! " when He died
  And His redeeming work begun.

And of the kings have warred and reigned,
  Since Jesu died, the King of Men,
And of the blood that earth hath stained,
  And of the streams must flow again.

And in the soldier's sacrifice,
  I saw the Christ's in its degree :
A sinful life—let it suffice,
  He laid it down for you and me.

For one a little cross of deal,
　　For One the Age-Enduring Tree ;
Yet each frail, faltering flesh did feel
In hands and feet the wounding steel ;
　　Each died that mankind might be free,
　　Each gave a life for you and me.

THE DRUM

" Come to me and I will give you flesh."
Old Pibrochadh.

COME !
Says the drum ;
    Though graves be hollow,
    Yet follow, follow :
Come !
Says the drum.

Life !
Shrills the fife,
Is in strife—
Leave love and wife :
Come !
Says the drum.

Ripe !
Screams the pipe,
    Is the field—
    Swords and not sickles wield :
Come !
Says the drum.

The drum
Says, Come !
    Though graves be hollow,
    Yet follow, follow :
Come !
Says the drum.

SOLDIER, SOLDIER

Wastrel, wastrel, standing in the street,
Billy-cock upon your head ; boots that
show your feet.

Rookie, rookie, not too broad of chest,
But game to do your bloomin' bit with
the bloomin' best.

Rookie, rookie, growling at the grub ;
Loth to wash behind the ears when you
take your tub.

Rookie, rookie, licking into shape—
Thirty-six inch round the buff showing by
the tape.

Rookie, rookie, boots and buttons clean ;
Mustachios waxing stronger ; military
mien.

Rookie, rookie, drilling in the square,
Britain's ancient glory in your martial air.

Rookie, rookie, swagger-stick to twirl ;
Waving hands to serving maids ; walking
   out the girl.

Soldier, soldier, ordered to the front,
Marching forward eager-eyed, keen to bear
   the brunt.

Soldier, soldier, bidding her good-bye—
" When I come back I'll marry you, so,
   darling, don't you cry ! "

Soldier, soldier, sailing in the ships,
Cigarettes and curious oaths betwixt your
   boyish lips.

Soldier, soldier, standing in the trench ;
Wading through the mud and mire,
   stifling in the stench.

Soldier, soldier, 'mid the din and dirt,
More than monastic tortures moving in
   your shirt.

Soldier, soldier, facing shot and shell ;
Jesting as you gaze within the open Gate
   of Hell.

Soldier, soldier, charging on the foe,
With your comrade's dying cry to urge
  you as you go.

Soldier, soldier, stilly lying dead,
With a dum-dum bullet through your
  dunder head.

Soldier, soldier, with a smile of grace,
Breaking through the grime and grit on
  your blood-swept face.

Soldier, soldier, sound will be your sleep,
You will never waken, though you hear
  her weep.

Soldier, soldier——
    How I love you !

"I CANNA SEE THE SERGEANT"

Those readers who have recollection of the drilling days of the 4th Battalion Black Watch may remember to have heard some words—often, fortunately, not entirely intelligible—which we rendered lustily as a marching song, to the Gaelic melody, " Horo My Nut-Brown Maiden." In these strenuous and sad times the phrase, " I Canna See the Sergeant," which formed the owre-turn o' the sang, has often assumed a new and deeper significance.

I CANNA see the sergeant,
I canna see the sergeant,
I canna—see the—sergeant,*
   He's owre far awa'.
Bring the wee chap nearer,
Bring the wee chap nearer,
O bring the—wee chap—nearer—
   He's owre bloomin' sma'.

We canna see the sergeant,
The five foot five inch sergeant,

* To be sung in staccato fashion.

We canna—see the—sergeant
    For smoke, and shell, and a'—
Now we can see him clearer,
Now we can see him nearer—
Upon the topmost parapet
    He's foremost o' us a' !

We canna see the sergeant,
The sma', stout-hearted sergeant,
We canna—see the—sergeant,
    He's dead and gone awa'.
Bring the wee chap nearer,
Bring the wee chap nearer,
O, he has grown the dearer
    Now that he's far awa' !

"WHEN WE REMEMBERED——"

THINK not, far friends, that we forget,
  In these red realms of wrack and rue,
The white cliffs round our England set,
  The Channel waters white and blue.

Think not, that on this smiling plain,
    Where, snake-like coiled, the trenches
      lie,
In dreams we do not see again
    Our bleak hills buttressing the sky.

Think not, within the grim, grey lines,
  Haunted by gaunt and grimy men,
Comes no cool chaunting of the pines
  That guard one well-remembered glen.

By black hearths in the broken farm,
  Bethink ye we remember not
The fire-glow, welcoming and warm,
    Which lights the path to one loved
      cot ?—
    Bethink ye we remember not ?

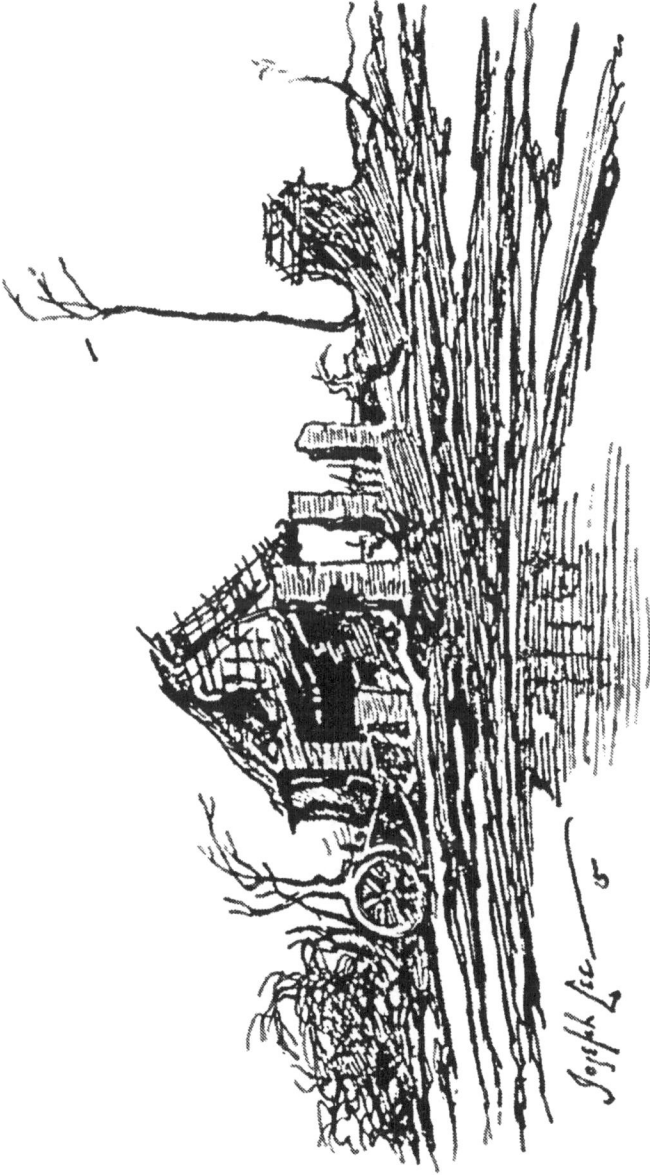

By black hearths in the broken farm.

—" When we Remembered——"

Joseph Lee

Here, where the ruined chapels raise
  Their blackened beams against the blue,
Comes echo of the hymn of praise
  Sung by our home-folk, leal and true.

Here, by the stile, where lovers stood,
  And strong hands laboured with the
    sheaves,
Where are dear drops of human blood
  As crimson as the poppy leaves ;

Here, where the ripened harvests rot—
  Where rot an hundred ungraved men,
Bethink ye we remember not
  The little Croft beneath the Ben ?
Bethink ye we have aught forgot ?
Bethink ye we remember not ?

BROKEN TREES AT ERICHT REDOUBT

THE HOME-COMING

WHEN this blast is over-blown,
  And the beacon fires shall burn,
    And in the street
    Is the sound of feet—
They also shall return.

When the bells shall rock and ring,
  When the flags shall flutter free,
    And the choirs shall sing,
    " God save our King "—
They shall be there to see.

When the brazen bands shall play,
  And the silver trumpets blow,
    And the soldiers come
    To the tuck of drum—
They shall be there also.

44

When that which was lost is found ;
  When each shall have claimed his kin,
    Fear not they shall miss
    Mother's clasp, maiden's kiss—
  For no strange soil might hold them in.

When Te Deums seek the skies,
  When the Organ shakes the Dome,
    A dead man shall stand
    At each live man's hand—
  For they also have come home.

THE MIRROR

To N. S., on the gift of a Metal Mirror received in
the trenches.

WHEN in this burnished steel I trace
My own begrimed and hair-grown face,
And, as of old, still smile to see
Some of the boy unquelled in me :

I also vision a fair lawn,
O'er which a placid sky is drawn,
While the broad firth flows at our feet—
For heaven itself a mirror meet :

A rosy copse, a roseate sky,
And we together, you and I,
In the garden at the cool of e'en,
Talking of dear dead things have been ;

Turning our dearly-boughten store
Of Memories, o'er and o'er and o'er—
So fragrant that each well might be
Rose petal from life's thorny tree—
Till full hearts fountain into tears
To vivify these long-dead years !

46

When in this shining steel I trace
My own begrimed and hair-grown face ;
A magic impress—I shall see
The smile of him who sent it me !

TYPICAL BARN BILLET

THE BAYONET

THE rifle bullet ranges far,
  The bursting shell seeks wide,
The mortar and machine guns are
  Both trusty friends and tried ;
But the swiftest weapon in the war
  Is the steel swings by my side.

The rifle rings out sharp and clear,
  The " 75 " can speak,
And viciously upon the ear
  Sound "swish-bang" and "pip-squeak,"
But the bayonet is the Silent Fear
  In this game of hide-and-seek.

The bullet speeds with wail and sob,
  The shrapnel showers its hails,
But the keen-edged bayonet point can
    probe
  Where the leaden pellet fails ;
And the " white arm " finishes the job—
  And dead men tell no tales !

The mortar gun is full of ire
  When once ye do begin it,
The facile mitrailleuse can fire
  Seven hundred rounds a minute,
But " La Rosalie " will never tire
  When once her finger's in it.

The blade upon the barrel clicks
  When the battle is begun,
And often has the Captain's " Fix ! "
  Carried us out o' one ;
Then thrust and parry—these the tricks
  By which the trench is won.

With thrust and parry, lunge and point,
  Point, parry, lunge, and thrust ;
Our knees seem going at the joint,
  Our hearts beat fit to burst—
And then—may Christ our souls aroint,—
  We stab at what seems accurst !—Ugh !

The rifle bullet ranges far,
  The bursting shell seeks wide,
The mortar and machine guns are
  Both trusty tools and tried ;
But the surest weapon in the war
  Is the steel swings by my side !

"STAY-AT-HOME HEARTS ARE BEST"—NOT 'ALF

THE men who stay at home at ease,
And go to bed just when they please,
Have lots o' baccy and o' beer,
And yet—I'd rather be out here !

The chaps who stay at home and dine
Have heaps of wictuals and o' wine,
With walnuts—shelled—and all good
    cheer—
It's better to be shelled out here !
                    (Swish—bang !)

The men who stay at home at ease
Need never try to wash their knees
In dixie* lids—yet never fear,
I'd rather far be dirty here !

       * A mess tin—very literally.

The chaps at home they earn good pay,
And don clean linen every day,
While my shirt runs—its wild career !
Yet—rather I'd be lousy here !

                (Yes, even that !)

The chaps who stay—the lucky dogs !—
Can stroll around in tailored togs,
While my make-up is something queer—
Yet—better be a scarecrow here !

The chaps who stay at home and play
At tennis through a summer day,
Need ne'er fall bleeding to the rear—
And yet—I'd rather play out here !

Sweet-hearting ?—ah ! you lucky chaps
Who go a-wooing—well, perhaps,
Unless I get a nasty whack,
I'll get a girl when I go back.

Why, yes, who knows ? there still might be
Some girl to love a bloke like me ;
There's Dolly—would she drop a tear
If I went under over here ?

The men who live at home at ease,
May list—then 'LIST—just as they please,
For me, by Christ ! my conscience clear,
I think I'd rather die out here !

                    (Stretcher-bearers !)

CORPORAL, GURKHA REGIMENT

INVOCATION : NIGHT IN THE TRENCHES

CREATOR of the stars
    Great and Little Bear—
    Have us in Thy care.

Thou who set Orion,
    Watch and ward to keep—
    Guard a soldier's sleep.

Hand that swung the Spheres,
    Strawed the Pleiades—
    Have pity upon these.

Hand that sways the plough ;
    Will that stays the Pole—
Sow thy good seed now,
    Guide an errant soul.

LA CROIX ROUGE

A Wayside Calvary in Flanders.

Two thousand years since Christ was
    crucified ;
Since thorn and nail did torment that
    frail flesh :
        Again I see
        Him hangéd on a tree,
And crucified afresh !

Once more that darkness over all the land;
The graves—*the graves are full*—they
    give not up their dead :
        The bitter cup
        Is lifted up,
The crown pierces His head.

The scourging rod, the mocking reed are
    His,
The veritable Son of Man and God ;
        Through feet and hands
        The iron stands,
The Cross is red with blood.

Barabbas is released unto the World ;
   The thieves—*the thieves are unrepentant*
      both—
         With swords and staves
         A crowd of knaves
   Come forth with jest and oath.

Again the brutal soldiery cast lots ;
   The earth is rent with wrath, and rack,
      and rue,
         Comes like a sigh
         That lonely cry :
   " They know not what they do ! "

Thou Kaiser, who hast crucified thy
      Christ ;
   Judas, Pilatus, Peter—three in one !
         Who shall it be
         Shall say to thee :
   Servant, thy work well done ?

For thirty pieces Judas sold his Lord,
   And Peter but denied his Master thrice ;
         And Pilate stands
         With washen hands—
   Princeling, what was thy price ?

E

Better, O Cæsar—Caiaphas, High Priest,
  With all thy servile Scribes and Phari-
    sees—
        Thou'dst ne'er been born
        Than put to scorn
One of the least of these !

Proud Kaiser, who has drowned the world
  in tears,
  And deluged all the earth with reddest
    rain—
        Christ's brow is torn
        With crown of thorn—
Thine bears the brand of Cain !

O King in name, who might have been in
  deed,
  Who chose the darkness rather than the
    light :
        I see thee go
        Forth from thy foe—
And it is night !

"WHEN THE ARMADA SAILED FROM SPAIN"

"God blew with His winds, and they were scattered."—Medal struck to commemorate defeat of the Armada.

WHEN the Armada sailed from Spain,
And launched its might upon the main,
    Bold Drake put out from Plymouth
    Hoe,
    And God's great wind began to blow—
    And it was scattered ;
    Well, what was then, brave boys,
    Will be again, brave, bully boys.
Aye ! What was then will be again !

When Wellington with his brave few
Met Buonaparte at Waterloo,
    The British bayonets drove Nap, back
    To St. Helena's lonely rack,
    Broken and battered ;
    Our steel's as true, brave boys,
    Our blood's as blue, brave, bully boys,
And Britain trusts to me and you !

Yet oft I've sheltered, snug and warm,
Within that friendly old French farm!
—"The Billet."

THE BILLET

A ROOF that hardly holds the rain ;
Walls shaking to the hurricane ;
Great doors upon their hinges creaking ;
Great rats upon the rafters squeaking—
A midden in the courtyard reeking—
Yet oft I've sheltered, snug and warm,
Within that friendly old French farm !

To trudge in from the soaking trench—
The blasts that bite, the rains that drench—
To loosen off your ponderous pack,
To drop the harness from your back,
Deliberate pull each muddy boot
From each benumbed, frost-bitten foot ;
To wrap your body in your blanket,
To mutter o'er a " Lord be thankit ! "
Sink out of sight below the straw,
Then—Owre the hills and far awa' !

*　　　*　　　*　　　*　　　*

Perchance to waken from your sleep,
And hear the big guns growling deep,

Turn on your side, but breathe a prayer
For the beggars you have left up " there."

Then in the morn to stretch your legs,
And hear the hens cluck o'er their eggs ;
And chanticleer's bestirring blare ;
The whinnying of the Captain's mare ;
Contented lowing of the kine,
Complacent grunting of the swine ;
Chirping of birds beneath the eaves,
Whisper of winds among the leaves,
And—sound that soul of man rejoices—
.he pleasant hum of women's voices—
With all the cheery dins that be
In a farmyard community ;
While sunlight bursting thro' the thatch
Burns in the black barn, patch and patch.

But now, your eyes and ears you ope—
The pipes are skirling, " Johnnie Cope "—*

There is something slightly sardonic in the
fact that the old Jacobite rant, " Hey, Johnnie
Cope, are ye waukin' yet ? " which was used for
the berousing and belabouring of the Whigs, should
now do duty as Reveille to a Highland regiment.
So, at least, it seems to one at seven o'clock of a
cold winter's morning !

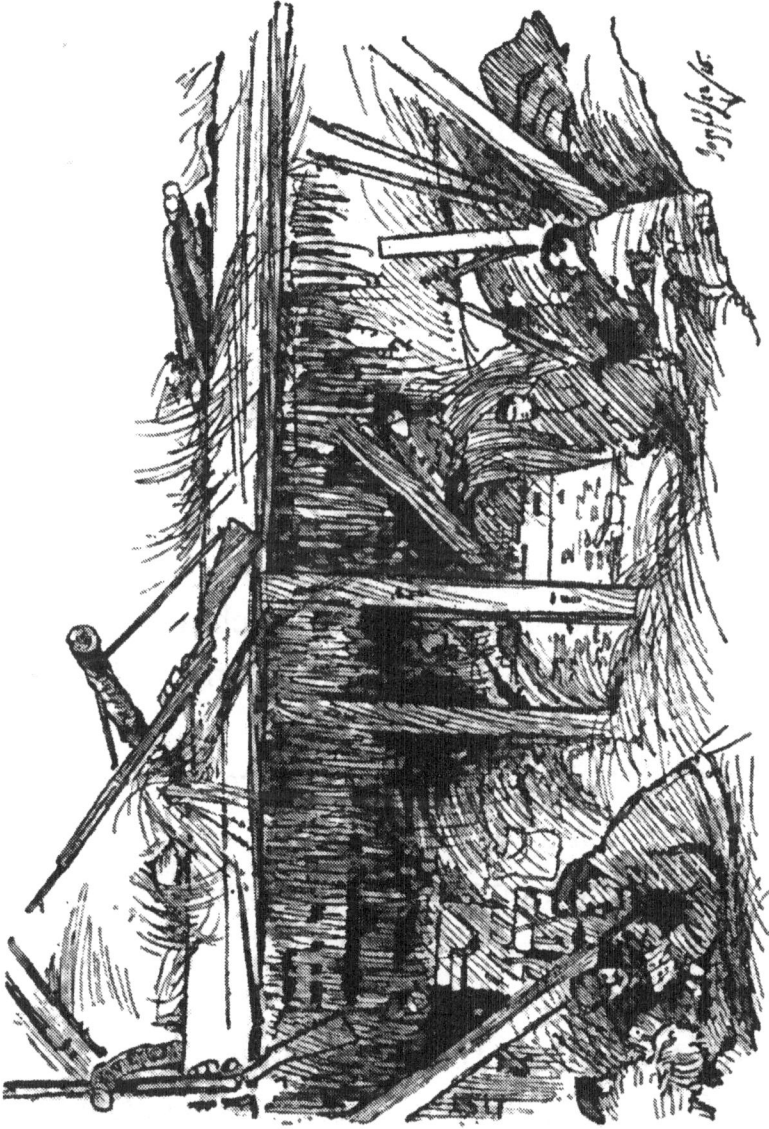

INTERIOR OF THE BARN.

—"The Billet."

And you arise to toil and trouble,
And certainly to " double ! double ! "—
Of the day's drills, most grudged of all,
That lagging hour called " physical ! "

Breakfast, of tea, and bread, and ham,
With just a colouring of jam ;
Or, if you have the sous to pay,
A feast of *œufs* and *café-au-lait.*

Comes ten o'clock and we fall in,
With rifle cleaned, and shaven chin ;
Once more we work the " manual "
    through,
And then " drill in platoons " we do
Till one, or maybe even two.
At last " cook-house " the pipers play,
And so we dine as best we may.

And now a shout that never fails
To fetch us forth, " Here come the
    mails ! "—
While one rejoices, t'other rails

Because he has received no letter—
Next time the Fates may use him better !

Then comes an hour beneath a tree,
With " Omar Khayyam " on your knee,
While wanton winds, in idle sport,
Bombard you after harmless sort
With apple blossoms from the bough—
Ah ! here is Paradise enow !

'Tis now that mystic hour of night
When—parcels open—no respite
Is given to cake, sweetmeat, sardine ;
Our zest would turn a gourmet green
With envy, could he only see
The meal out here, that's yclept " tea."

The night has come, and all are hearty,
Being exempt from a " working-party " :
And so we gather round the fire
To chat, and presently conspire
To pass an hour with song and story—
The grave, the gay, ghostly or gory,—

A tale, let's say, both weird and fierce,
By Allan Poe or Ambrose Bierce,*
Then Skerry—Peace be to his Shade !—
May play us Gounod's " Serenade,"
And, gazing thro' the broken beams,
Perchance we see the starry gleams.

    *   *   *   *   *

But " Lights-out ! " sounds ; " Good
    nights " are said,
And so we bundle off to bed.

Sweet dreams infest each drowsy head
And kindly Ghosts that work no harm
Flit round about that old French farm !

* The greatest compliment I ever received to my
power as a story-teller was paid me by a comrade,
who, on the morning after the recital of Bierce's
" The Middle Toe of the Right Foot," presented me
with a small model of a human foot, minus a toe,
which he had executed in the wax of a candle !

A GHOST STORY AT THE FRONT

A tale, let's say, both weird and fierce,
By Allan Poe or Ambrose Bierce.

—"The Billet.'

NOCTURNALS

Tommy's Night Thoughts in the Trenches.

I

I WONDER are there stupid wars
In any of them other stars ?—
　　　Kaisers and Kings,
　　　And mix o' things,
　　　And all this mess ?—
　　　Not 'alf, I guess,
Not even in yon ruddy Mars.

II

As I stamp my feet to keep them hot,
　　When a' the trench is still,
O, I wad gi'e a hell o' a lot
　　For the sight o' a Scottish hill,
　　　For the clasp o' a Scottish lassie's
　　　　waist,
　　　And—weel—just to say a little taste
O' a guid auld Scottish gill !

66

III

Lord of the Night, be near me now,
Strength for my Heart, Shield for my
   Brow ;
And when Thy white Light returns again—
Lord of the Day, be with me then.

IV

7.55 A.M.

A funny world—
    There's him,
    And me,
Both thirstin', be it understood,
To draw the other's bleedin' blood—
    And yet,
    I'd bet
    A bob—and win it—
    That at this minute,
    Both he,
    And me,
Are thirstin' most—to draw our dixie lid
    O' TEA !

V

SUMMING UP !

When our wrath is expended,
When the world war is ended,
    It seems like to me
    That this old earth will be
More broken than mended.

VI

BON VOYAGE !

The sky is the sea,
    And ships are the clouds,
And dead sailor men
    Swing into the shrouds—
Heigh-ho ! Some day
I shall sail far away !

THE COMBAT

"For I am fearfully and wonderfully made."

I with my mouth must munch my food,
Even as the monster in the wood,
And yet, dear heart, my lips to thine
Have clung in ecstasies divine !

I feel my ribs like prison-bars,
And still, I comprehend the stars ;
Through the white mas'nry of my bones
A sleepless spirit stalks and groans !

This pulsing heart is all afire
With passion and with wild desire,
And still, I turn dim yearning eyes
Thrice daily to the unanswering skies,

I have in me to burn and slay—
And yet a little child will lay
Its soft warm cheek upon my cheek,
And I, as it, am mild and meek !

The hunger of the wolf I have,
And yet, I hunger most for love,
And often have I wept to scan
The misery of my brother-man.

I hear, within the forest wild,
A whispering : *Thou art our child !*
And yet, again I hear a call
Within the vast Cathedral.

Oft have I clasped thee in my arms,
And loved thee for thy woman's charms ;
Yet have I sought, and seemed to see
And love, a woman's *soul* in thee !

The fleshly lust, the pride of life,
The joyaunce in a selfish strife,
The din of battle in my ear—
And yet a still small voice I hear !

I would not do the thing I would,
I shun the evil, seek the good ;
Comes prompting from the past : You
    must !
And pulls me backward in the dust.

My hands are clawed to clutch and keep ;
My eyes grow heavy unto sleep,
I crouch beneath a poor roof-tree,
I wake—and I am still with Thee.

I know that when I come to die,
My bones all strawed about shall lie ;
The hand that fashioned shall annul
This cunning sculpture of my skull.

O Thou behind that outmost star,
Have mercy if Thy plans we mar,
For lo ! we know not what we are !

I with my mouth must munch my food
Like uncouth creatures in the wood,
Yet from my lips what prayers arise
Alway to the unanswering skies !

F

THE MOUTH-ORGAN

WHEN drum and fife are silent,
  When the pipes are packed away,
    And the soldiers go
    Too near the foe
  For the bugle's noisy bray ;
When our haversacks are heavy,
  And our packs like Christian's load,
    Then Jimmy Morgan*
    Plays his old mouth-organ,
  To cheer us on our road.
    " It's a long, long way to Tipperary—"

* Though for obvious reasons of rhyme I have
here ventured to appropriate the classic name
" Jimmy Morgan," nevertheless the best mouth-
organist in D Company, if not in the battalion, is
2203 Private William Brough. He informs me that
his present instrument is something the worse for
wear.

When by the shrunken river
  Reclined the great god Pan,
      And to his needs,
      Cut down the reeds—
And music first began ;
Then all mankind did marvel
  At a melody so sweet ;
      But when Jimmy Morgan
      Plays his old mouth-organ,
Even Pan takes second seat !

When Orpheus, of old time,
  Did strike his magic lute,
      He lorded it,
      As he thought fit,
O'er boulder, bird, and brute ;
And great trees were uprooted,
  And *root*-marched, so to say,
      But when Jimmy Morgan
      Plays his old mouth-organ,
You should see us march away.

When the Piper Pied of Hamelin,
  In the legend of renown,
    His pipe did play,
    He charmed away
The children from the town :
But behold our whole Battalion—
  To the joy of wife and wench—
    Led by Jimmy Morgan,
    And his old mouth-organ,
March forward to the trench.
    " *Here we are, here we are, here we*
      are again ! "

O, an overture by Wagner
  Strikes sweetly on mine ear,
    And that noble three,
    Brahms, Bach, and Bee-
thoven, I love to hear ;
But when the rains are falling,
  And when the roads are long,
    Give me Jimmy Morgan
    And his old mouth-organ
To lead our little song.
    " *A-roving, a-roving ; we'll gang*
      nae mair a-roving ! "

Sometimes he pipes us grave notes,
  Sometimes he pipes us gay ;
      Till broken feet
      Take up the beat
Of quick-step or Strathspey :
But he plays upon our heart-strings
  When he plays a Scottish tune—
      Hear Jimmy Morgan
      And his old mouth-organ
At " The Banks o' Bonnie Doon " !

He has a twist upon his mouth,
  A twinkle in his e'e ;
      A roguish air,
      A deil-ma-care,
  Like the Piper o' Dundee :
Faith ! we would dance thro' half o'
    France,
  And a' the trenches carry,
      If Jimmy Morgan
      On his old mouth-organ,
  Did but give us " Annie Laurie " !

And when the war is over—
  The war we mean to win—
    And Kaiser Bill
    Has had his pill,
  And we boys march thro' Berlin ;
" Unter den Linden " going,
  We'll need no pipes to blow—
    Just Jimmy Morgan
    And his old mouth-organ,
  Leading us as we go !
    —" *Highland   laddie,   Highland
    laddie ; whar hae you been a'
    the day ?* " *

And when this life is ended,
  And Morgan gone aloft,
    He will not carp
    Tho' he get no harp,
  Nor trumpet sweet and soft ;
But if there be a place for him
  In the Angelic choir,
    Give Jimmy Morgan
    His old mouth-organ,
  And he'll play and never tire.

  * The Regimental March of the Black Watch.

THE MOTHER

" Mother o' mine ; O Mother o' mine."

MY mother rose from her grave last night,
  And bent above my bed,
And laid a warm kiss on my lips,
  A cool hand on my head ;
And, " Come to me, and come to me,
  My bonnie boy," she said.

*   *   *   *   *

And when they found him at the dawn,
  His brow with blood defiled,
And gently laid him in the earth,
  They wondered that he smiled.

TOMMY AND FRITZ

HE hides behind his sand-bag,
  And I stand back o' mine ;
And sometimes he bellows, " Hullo, John
    Bull ! "
  And I hollers, " German swine ! "
And sometimes we both lose our bloomin'
    rag,
  And blaze all along the line.

Sometimes he whistles his 'Ymn of 'Ate,
  Or opens his mug to sing,
And when he gives us " Die Wacht am
    Rhein "
  I give 'im " God Save the King " ;
And then—we " get up the wind " again,
  And the bullets begin to ping—
(If we're in luck our machine gun nips
  A working squad on the wing.)

Sometimes he shouts, " Tommy, come
   over ! "
And we fellers bawl out, " Fritz,
If yer wants a good warm breakfast,
   Walk up and we'll give you fits ! "
And sometimes our great guns begin to
   growl,
   And blows his front line to bits.

And when our shrapnel has tore his wire,
   And his parapet shows a rent,
We over and pays him a friendly call
   With a bayonet—but no harm meant.
And he—well, when he's resuscitate,
   He returns us the compliment !

I stand behind my sand-bag,
   And he hides back o' his'en ;
And, but for our bloomin' uniforms,
   We might both be convicts in pris'n ;
And sometimes I loves him a little bit—
   And sometimes I 'ate like p'ison.

For sometimes I mutters " Belgium,"
  Or " Lusitani—a,"
And I slackens my bay'net in its sheath,
  And stiffens my lower jaw,
And " An eye for an eye ; a tooth for a
    tooth,"
  Is all I know of the Law.

But sometimes when things is quiet,
  And the old kindly stars come out,
I stand up behind my sand-bag,
  And think, " What's it all about ? "
And—tho' I'm a damned sight better nor
    him,
  Yet sometimes I have a doubt,
That if you got under his hide you would
    see
A bloke with a heart just the same's you
    and me !

THE BROKEN HEART

I FOUND a silver sixpence,
A sixpence, a sixpence,
I found a silver sixpence,
    And I brake it in twa ;
I gied it till a sodger,
A sodger, a sodger,
I gied it till a sodger,
    Before he gaed awa'.

I have a heart that's broken,
That's broken, that's broken ;
I bear a heart that's broken,
    That's broken in twa—
For I gied it till a sodger,
A sodger, a sodger,
I gied it till a sodger,
    Before he gaed awa' !

BIG GUNS

BIG guns baying,
  Baying thro' the night,
What are ye saying
  Of the fight ?
Who are ye slaying ?

Big guns booming,
  Booming thro' the night,
Who are ye dooming
  To endless glooming,
In each fell flight ?

Great guns growling,
  Growling till the day,
Like wild winds howling ;
  Like wild beasts prowling—
What is thy prey ?

Big guns baying,
  Baying thro' the night,
What are ye saying
  Of the fight ?—
Who are ye slaying ?

SUBIDAR MAJOR JOCUNDAR SINGH
69th PUNJABIS

PIOU-PIOU

The British Tommy Atkins to the French.

YOUR trousies is a funny red,
   Your tunic is a funny blue,
Your cap sets curious on your 'ead—
   And yet, by Gawd, your 'eart sits true,
      Piou-piou !

Your menu's even worse nor mine,
   Your pay a day is but a sou ;
But still, you blokes have broke the
   line—
   I'm proud to fight along o' you,
      Piou-piou !

Your lingo I do not compr-ee—
   A necessary word or two—
But, " deux bier's " enough for me,
   And here's the best o' health to you,
      Piou-piou !

PIOU-PIOU

MARCHING

Marching, marching,
  On the old-time track ;
    Soldier song upon my lip,
    Haversack upon my hip,
  Pack upon my back ;
    Linton on my left hand,
  On my right side Jack—
Marching, marching,
    Steel swung at my thigh,
Marching, marching,
    Who so gay as I ?
               (Left, left !)

Marching, marching,
  On the same old track ;
    Sorrow gnawing at my heart,
    Mem'ry piercing like a dart,
  Care perched on my back ;
    Linton on my left hand—
But, alas ! poor Jack !
Marching, marching,
    Quietly does he lie,
Marching, marching,
    Who so sad as I ?
             (Left, left—*LEFT* /)

HOLLOW TREE BIVOUAC

G

PICK AND SPADE

The Plaint of Tommy—aching.

Out here we call a spade a spade, and a shovel a
shovel—with embellishment!

PICK and spade,
Pick and spade,
Five hundred miles o' trench we've made,
Five hundred thousand sandbags laid
    Wi' pick and spade.

Pick and spade
Pick and spade,
My apron's tore, and my kilt is frayed,
And the hide off my horny hands is
    flayed—
I wish to Gawd on the farm I'd stayed
    Wi' pick and spade.

Pick and spade,
Pick and spade ;
What made the stoutest heart afraid ?—
When the S.M. shoved in his head and
    said :

" The whole of the fourteenth platoon
    will parade
        Wi' pick and spade ! "

    Pick and spade,
    Pick and spade,
Every man jack of us all of a trade ;
" Fall in the blokes o' the Navvy's
    Brigade,
        Wi' pick and spade ! "

    Pick and spade,
    Pick and spade,
Thingumabob 90° in the shade ;
On thro' the mud and the muck we
    wade—
A dead man's skull—and I've broken the
    blade
        O' my bluidy old spade !

    Pick and spade,
    Pick and spade ;
This is the way that the War Game's
    played—
Bill's got hit i' the leg and is off to First
    Aid—

" I wish to 'Eaven 't had been me ! " I
    prayed :
        " Damn this pick and spade ! "

        Pick and spade,
        Pick and spade,
I wish to Gawd that the blokes wi' red
    braid
Round their caps, for only a spell could
    be made
        To parade
        For a trick o' our trade
        Wi' the pick and spade !

SHEATH NOT THE SWORD

" Peace, peace, when there is no peace."

SHEATH not the Sword ere yet the strife
  is ended ;
Prate not of peace before proud wills
  are bended—
    Sheath not the Sword !

Sheath not the Sword ! What of thy
  valiant dead ?
'Twas not for this their rich hearts' blood
  was shed—
    Sheath not the Sword !

Sheath not the Sword ! Thousands our
  kinsmen stand
Waiting the issue in that Shadow land—
    Sheath not the Sword !

Sheath not the Sword ! Thousands thy
    kinsmen wait
To enter at thy need stern Death's dark
    gate——
        Sheath not the Sword !

Harden thy heart ! Stay not the slaying
    hand,
Till each, erect, stand in his cleanséd land—
        Sheath not the Sword !

Harden thy heart ! Withhold the pitying
    ear,
Until their Hymn of Hate turn to a cry of
    fear !——
        Sheath not the Sword !

CARRYING-PARTY

Time 10.30 p.m.   Place, Communication Trenches.

WIRE over'ead !
  Mud underfoot :
      Gawd, I'm into a hole,
      Pullin' the sole
  Right off'en me boot—
I wish I was dead !

Wire over'ead—
(My load weighs like lead)
  The night's black as 'ell ;
      I'm into a ditch—
      Ye son of a bitch !
  'Twas here Nelson fell—
  Bang ! There goes a shell—
I wish I was dead !

Wire over'ead !—
   Look out for the bridge !
      Hear ole Sergeant grunt,
       " Halt ! you there in front !
   They've lost touch at the ridge "—
I wish *I* was dead !

Wire over'ead !
   Wire underfoot !—
      There's Tim come to grief—
      Christ !—he's dumping the beef.
   Pull 'im out by the root :
I wish I was dead—
(To home blokes are in bed)—
Wish Ga wd I was dead !
       (*Stumbles and grumbles on.*)

SONG OF TRUE LOVERS

WHEN we two parted,
   It was a weeping rain ;
The sun shall shine upon the day
   That we two meet again.

When we two severed,
   The stream was drowned in mist ;
Upon that eve, with moonlight
   Its waters will be kiss'd.

When we two parted,
   It was an eerie wind ;
When I shall set my sail for home
   The breezes will be kind.

When we two parted,
   The trees stood gaunt and bare ;
They will be bourgeoning with Spring
   When next we wander there.

When we two parted,
　　The year was at its close ;
Some day, some day, the desert
　　Shall blossom as the rose.

When we two parted,
　　The days were full of pain ;
When next we meet, we meet, indeed,
　　Never to part again,
　　　　　Dear love,
　　Never to part again.

1815–1915

ONE HUNDRED YEARS AGO TO-DAY

TO MY GRANDFATHER
WHO FOUGHT AT WATERLOO

*Affectionately Dedicated to
my Four Paternal Aunts.*

ONCE more the unsheathed sword, once
    more the speeding shell ;
Once more unleashing of the Hounds of
    Hell ;
The Nations rage together, and again
The Kings are joined for battle on the
    plain ;
Old Europe armed goes forth to smite
    and slay,
Just as a Hundred Years to-day !

Grandsire, whom I have never seen, nor
  held whose hand,
Nor heard whose voice—stentorian in
  command—
From some Valhalla of the British dead
Perchance thou watchest where our lines
  are spread :
Strengthen my hand ; thy kinsman's
  heart inspire
With some spark of thy ancient martial
  fire—
May my steel be as keen, I pray,
As yours, a Hundred Years to-day !

Oft as a boy I strove to swing thy blade
From out the scabbard where it long had
  laid,
And fearful felt its edge—the notch,
  'twas said,
Was compliment from a dead Chasseur's
  head—
And all day waged the mimic fight,
Waiting for Blucher—and nurse !—and
  night :

Thank God ! and I see the children play
As I did—was it Yesterday ?

I hear your guns growl on through Spain,
And then, I hear them once again
Take up the old terrific tune
Upon that far-off Eighteenth June—
Mine ears have learned the measure well
At Festubert and Neuve Chapelle—
Our friends, forth with us in this fray,
Were foes a Hundred Years to-day !

When you rode through this war-racked
    land
Didst ever, prithee, kiss a hand
To Jeanne, Yvonne, Marcelle, Marie—
Grand-dames of those wave hands to me ?
Were girls as sportive and as gay ?—
Didst have the heart to say them Nay ?—
Was't easy parting with thy pay
A Hundred Years Ago to-day ?

*   *   *   *   *

Grandsire, whose good right hand is long
    since dust,
I hold the same true steel in sacred trust ;
From some Valhalla of the British dead
Perchance thou watchest where our lines
    are spread ;
Thou knewest whence should come the
    power
When dark the battle-clouds did lower—
May thy God be my shield and stay
As thine a Hundred Years to-day !

FLANDERS, 18th June, 1915.

REQUIEM

When the last voyage is ended,
　And the last sail is furled,
When the last blast is weathered,
　And the last bolt is hurled,
　　And there comes no more the sound
　　　of the old ship bell—
　　Sailor, sleep well !

When the Last Post is blown,
　And the last volley fired,
When the last sod is thrown,
　And the last Foe retired,
　　And thy last bivouac is made under
　　　the ground—
　　Soldier, sleep sound !

Lightning Source UK Ltd.
Milton Keynes UK
UKOW07n0849171214

243255UK00008B/107/P